You'll Pay for This!

How We Can Afford a Great City for Everyone, Forever

Michel Durand-Wood

YOU'LL PAY FOR THIS!

How We Can Afford a Great City for Everyone, Forever

Michel Durand-Wood

GREAT PLAINS
PRESS

Copyright © 2025 Michel Durand-Wood

Great Plains Press
320 Rosedale Ave
Winnipeg, MB R3L 1L8
www.greatplainspress.ca

All rights reserved. No part of this publication may be reproduced or transmitted in any form or in any means, or stored in a database and retrieval system, without the prior written permission of Great Plains Publications, or, in the case of photocopying or other reprographic copying, a license from Access Copyright (Canadian Copyright Licensing Agency), 1 Yonge Street, Suite 1900, Toronto, Ontario, Canada, M5E 1E5.

Great Plains Publications gratefully acknowledges the financial support provided for its publishing program by the Government of Canada through the Canada Book Fund; the Canada Council for the Arts; the Province of Manitoba through the Book Publishing Tax Credit and the Book Publisher Marketing Assistance Program; and the Manitoba Arts Council.

Design & Typography by Electric Monk Media
Printed in Canada by Friesens

Library and Archives Canada Cataloguing in Publication

Title: You'll pay for this : how we can afford a great city for everyone, forever / Michel Durand-Wood.
Other titles: You will pay for this
Names: Durand-Wood, Michel, author.
Description: Series statement: The city project ; 1
Identifiers: Canadiana (print) 20250103915 | Canadiana (ebook) 20250103923 | ISBN 9781773371344
 (softcover) | ISBN 9781773371375 (EPUB)
Subjects: LCSH: City planning—Economic aspects. | LCSH: Cities and towns—Growth—Economic aspects. | LCSH: Urbanization—Economic aspects. | LCSH: Sustainable urban development—Economic aspects.
Classification: LCC HT166 .D87 2025 | DDC 307.1/16—dc23

Table of Contents

Introduction	6
Chapter 1: Where Have All the Flowers Gone?	12
Chapter 2: What's a Butfor?	20
Chapter 3: It's Like Deja Vu All Over Again	30
Chapter 4: Bond, Municipal Bond	43
Chapter 5: There's No Accounting for Taste	56
Chapter 6: Til Debt Do Us Part	67
Chapter 7: Back to the Future	70
Chapter 8: The Ghosts of Budgets Past	76
Chapter 9: Let's Make a Deal!	85
Chapter 10: One Free Lunch, Please!	96
Chapter 11: Night of the Living Debt: Revenge of the Zombies	104
Chapter 12: All Bezzle, No Steak	113
Chapter 14: What Happened to Chapter 13?	122
Chapter 15: Connecting the Dots	124
Chapter 16: Welcome to the 1%!	136
Author's Note	142
Recommended Resources	146

Introduction

If you're reading this, you probably care about your city. I do too, that's why I wrote this book. Sorry, that was confusing. I wrote this book because I care about *my* city. I didn't write it because you care about *your* city. I mean, I'm really glad you care about your city, and I wish your city well, but it's not why I wrote this book.

Eesh, not off to a great start … one paragraph in and I've already hurt your feelings. I'm sorry, this is the first time I've written a book. Can we start over?

If you're reading this, you've noticed that Winnipeg, like most other cities in North America, is facing significant challenges these days. And, like me, you've noticed that it's been happening for a while: the service cuts, the tax increases, the neglected infrastructure.

Whether your city is Winnipeg, or some other city facing the same challenges, you've likely asked yourself why the city never seems to have the money to do what it's supposed to do.

From budget to budget, each year seems to be an exercise in deciding which service to cut, which pool to close, which library hours to shorten, which infrastructure to neglect, how much of a tax increase to give.

But even with all those cuts, even with the tax increases, and even with all that new growth on the edges of the city, we never seem to get ahead. Things definitely seem like they're trending for the worse.

Why is that? And in all its 150-year history, was it always like this?

Yikes, that's too depressing a start for a book. Especially for one that's going to be about municipal finance. Municipal finance is supposed to be fun, don't you think? Sorry, let me try again.

If you're reading this, you're probably not an accountant. I know that because most people aren't accountants.

That might seem obvious, in the same sense as most people aren't a professional hockey player, or the billionaire owner of a tech company, or a superhero in a red-and-blue spandex bodysuit with spider-like powers who fights crime at night to the ire of the local newspaper editor.

Clearly, those are all a very small proportion of the total population. It's the same for accountants.

In fact, Certified Professional Accountants Canada (CPA Canada) reports having 210,000 members as of 2024. Given that the total population of Canada is estimated by Statistics Canada to be just over 41 million, that means only 0.5% of Canadians are accountants.

It's similar in the United States. The US Bureau of Labor Statistics estimates that there are 1,562,000 accounting jobs in the country. Out of a population of 335 million, that gives us just a bit less than 0.5% of Americans being accountants.

So since 99.5% of you out there aren't accountants, I wasn't really going out on a limb, was I?

Now, by grouping accountants in with superheroes, I'm not necessarily saying that accountants *are* superheroes.

I mean, I'm not *not* saying it. Who knows what spandex lurks in the closets of accountants?

But what I am saying is that finance is hard for most people, and that for those who can understand it, well, it's almost like having a superpower.

And even if we assume that an equal number of people who currently aren't accountants understand finance as well as accountants do, that still leaves 99% of all people who don't.

That's a lot of us.

10 You'll Pay For This!

I'll tell you why that's important. Our city, all cities actually, provides a lot of services that are critical to our lives and well-being. It provides clean drinking water and sewage treatment, public safety, sanitation, transportation, and more. It also provides quality-of-life amenities like recreation options, libraries, and greenspaces.

But those things cost money. And if our city is going to be able to keep providing not only the quality-of-life services, but the critical, life-sustaining ones too, we're going to need to make sure that money is there. Not only today, not only tomorrow, but forever.

Unfortunately, if 99% of people in general don't have a firm grasp of city finance, or any finance, how can we be sure?

After all, that means that, despite their very best intentions, 99% of the voting public, 99% of local journalists reporting on city issues, 99% of city staff, and 99% of council members likely don't know, nor have any way to check either.

That's not anyone's fault. But it should still be addressed. Luckily, it's not that it can't be understood. Despite what you think, or what you may have been told, it's not too hard for the average person to understand. It's just never been properly explained to you. Until now.

So buckle up, friends. Using Winnipeg as a case study, we're going to take a literary trip together to learn to follow the money, how to make sure this city (or your city!) can afford to be the best it can be, and how to continue to pay for it for all time. No spandex necessary. (Although it's fine if you want to).

And on the off chance that you actually are an accountant, read on anyway! Maybe you'll still learn a new twist on an old concept. At the very least, you don't want to be left out of book club! The snacks are always so delicious.

Chapter 1

Where Have All the Flowers Gone?

I often think about the gardener in Elmwood Park.

If you don't know it, Elmwood Park is a small neighbourhood park. Locals like me lovingly refer to it as Roxy Park, even though that's never actually been its official name. It's always been Elmwood Park.

Aside from having two names—the real one and the one people actually use—it also has a sandbox, an aging wading pool, a swing set and play structure, a couple of benches, and an open area that can serve for pickup games of soccer, outdoor movie nights or winter skating.

Like so many places in the city, it's definitely looking a little worse for wear, a result of decades of neglect from municipal budget cuts.

Many of the structures are nearing, or well past, the end of their useful lives. The lighting is insufficient, and there are often weeds, and garbage, and overgrown brush.

But many of my neighbours pick up garbage there on their daily walks, or spend time during the summer pulling weeds, planting community gardens, and adding public art. It's where children play and dogs are walked.

As a park, it's pretty unremarkable, but it's ours and we love it.

But for nearly sixty years starting in the early 1900s, Elmwood Park was a shining gem. My next-door neighbour, who has lived here since their childhood in the 1940s, remembers it being a common location for people taking wedding photos. No doubt because, until the mid-1960s, the park had a full-time gardener who maintained it and planted up to 1,200 flowers every spring. The park also had a lily pond and fountain, a lot more seating, and amenities such as barbeque pits.

It was picture-perfect, worthy of a postcard. I know because I actually found a literal postcard from the 1940s featuring Elmwood Park.

I know, right? Hard to believe ol' Roxy Park used to be that nice.

But more importantly, that it wasn't the only one. A 1941 transportation map from the Winnipeg Electric Company (which operated the city's streetcars at the time) had this to say:

> Large parks such as Assiniboine and Kildonan are well-known but there are many other smaller parks distinct in their own special attractions, which are not so generally used by the citizens at large. A corner of one such park is pictured here. This quiet lily pool is in Elmwood Park on the banks of the Red River at Glenwood Crescent ... There are scores of other small parks all within easy reach by street car or bus.

You read that right. Scores. Scores!

If Abe Lincoln has taught us anything, it's that a score is twenty. And our city once had, not one score, but multiple scores (with an "s") of small neighbourhood parks that looked like this. Maybe not four score and seven, but scores nonetheless.

The point I'm trying to emphasize here is that while this might seem outright luxurious to us today, there was a time in our city's history, which lasted many, many decades, when we could afford this. We could afford to pay staff to make even our small neighbourhood parks breathtakingly beautiful.

And we continued to afford it through a World War, a global influenza epidemic, a general strike, the Great Depression, a second World War, and a flood of the century. But then in the mid-1960s, all of a sudden, we had to start letting go of our park gardeners. What gives? Instead of finding out the cause of our budget crunch, we just cut some services. After all, gardeners are a nice-to-have, not critical to our city like roads are, right? And so it started, our journey towards decades of necessary cuts into services that we used to be able to afford.

Catherine Macdonald's 1995 book, *A City at Leisure: An Illustrated History of Parks and Recreation Services in Winnipeg*, has an entire chapter titled "Hard Choices: The Eighties and Nineties." In it, she explains that:

> The necessity of funding these development schemes while also maintaining other needed services caused the city to dig itself badly into debt. At the end of the eighties, the Parks and Recreation Department found itself faced with some difficult challenges.

Hard choices. Difficult challenges. We've been using these words with respect to our city budgets for so long, before a lot of us were even born, that it has become normalized to us. New budget, new budget cuts. Every year, we pay more taxes for fewer services.

And this is normal.

Yet today, it's about much more than gardeners: potholed

Where Have All the Flowers Gone?   17

streets we can never seem to get ahead of, decommissioned pools, the indefinite closure of the Arlington Bridge, the highest per capita debt in our city's history, and a rainy-day fund that is now empty.

Worse even is that financial decline has not been felt equally by everyone. The generations of service cuts have taken their toll on our most vulnerable neighbours. And it's gotten to the point that it's impossible to look away, with some prominent Winnipeggers even going as far as calling it a humanitarian crisis.

It would be wrong to blame the COVID-19 pandemic. It may have accelerated the decline, but it didn't cause it. As we can see, this was happening well before then. At least since we were forced to lay off the gardener at Elmwood Park.

So then, why is it that every year that I've been alive, and even for a decade before that, we have had to make new cuts? How is it that, despite 150 years of consecutive balanced operating budgets (as is mandated by provincial law), and despite a growing population, we can afford less and less with each passing year?

That's the question I was trying to answer when I started digging into city finance nearly a decade ago. And it's the journey I'm hoping to take you on with this book.

We deserve better than to live in a city that is in constant decline. If I'm being honest, I'd like to see a gardener in Elmwood Park again at some point. And I'm sure you can easily think of several things in your neighbourhood you'd like to see improved, if the money was there for it.

We can get there. It obviously wasn't always like this, and so it doesn't have to continue to be. But for us to change the path forward, we'll need to follow the money. And not only follow it, but understand it.

Now I know that learning about city finance sounds scary, or boring, or anxiety-inducing, or any number of other negative emotions. Kinda like watching a documentary on paint drying, or worse, *not* being able to watch it because your wi-fi is down.

But trust me when I tell you that anyone can understand municipal finance. Anyone. That includes your great-aunt Helga, the teenager next door who mows your lawn (Connor, I think?), and of course, you.

And not only can you do it, but you'll have fun doing it!

Sounds unbelievable, I know. Well, what if I told you there's wine involved?

I thought so. Let's get to it then!

And don't worry if you don't drink wine, because we'll also be whipping up a batch of super-fun grape punch. After all, Connor's thirsty too.

But before we get too ahead of ourselves, it's important to ask, what is a city *for* anyway?

Chapter 2

What's a Butfor?

I'm going to address the elephant in the room right now. Throughout this book, we're going to talk about stuff like money and profit, productivity and investment.

And using those kinds of words when talking about cities might irk some people. After all, a city is an order of government. It shouldn't turn a profit, because it isn't like a business … or is it?

No. No, it isn't.

But let's just put a pin in that for now. Just set it aside next to the butfor.

(Hehe, made you say it. A butfor is, well, let's just put second pin in *that*, and I'll come back to it.)

Before we go any further, no discussion about finance is complete without talking about value, in the sense of "value for money." But in a similar vein, we also have to talk about values, with an "s," in the sense of "what we care about." After all, since money is finite, one of the most basic financial decisions a city has to make is, "what should we spend our money on?"

You've likely already heard the Oscar Wilde quote about "a man who knows the price of everything and the value of nothing." It's a brilliant reminder that the cost of something, its price, isn't necessarily the same thing as its worth, or its value. And even though the word "valuation" is often used to mean "to put a price on," we can see all around us that not everything that has value can be, well, valued.

For example, how do you put a price on the love of a parent, the air we breathe, or not seeing any online spoilers for that show you're currently binging? They're so valuable as to be priceless.

The same can be said for many city services, like sanitation, sewer systems and clean drinking water. Sure, we can easily determine what those services *cost*, but what is their *value* in terms of public health, safety and convenience? What are they *worth*? In a sense, you could argue that as long as the cost of providing a service is less than what it's worth, then the city should provide that service. Otherwise, we shouldn't.

So that's it, right?

Well, in reality it's a bit more complicated than that.

Often, just putting a price on something can end up devaluing it. In their book, *Freakonomics*, Steven D. Levitt and Stephen J. Dubner recount a study of daycare centres that instituted fines for parents who picked up their children late. The number of late pickups promptly went up after the fines went in, since the cost of the fine was seen to be less than the value of the social stigma for being late. Even worse is that, once the fines were removed, the late pickups stayed high. The erosion of value of the stigma was permanent.

If the very act of putting a price on a city service to value it can make it less valuable, we may end up cutting services that were worthwhile before, but aren't as much anymore once they have a price put on them. And that may be irreversible once we measure it. Yikes!

On top of that, what something is worth will often differ from person to person. One person may care about access to a public pool more than the next person, while some other person thinks the pool has no value at all and should be closed. In a city, determining what that pool is "worth" becomes very difficult, if not impossible. Repeat that for every service a city provides, and you can see how we'd get nowhere fast.

And yet, over the past eight decades or so, that's precisely the approach we've taken. Whenever there hasn't been enough money for everything that we used to fund, it's been an exercise in prioritizing what to cut. Which services are more worthwhile than others? Which have more value?

Maybe you've heard of the three Ps: police, pipes and pavement. That phrase is the embodiment of this approach, distilling city services down to only three core services deemed to have the most value over all the others. If something needs to be cut, it's everything but these three.

Whether these three are ultimately the "right" three doesn't matter. Because if you don't address the underlying cause of why there isn't enough money to begin with, eventually, you have to face some even harder truths. Like, what happens when you don't have enough money for even the three Ps?

That's what we're facing today: overextended police budgets, sewer spills into the river, closed bridges, potholed streets.

So what now? You cut again, prioritizing the most "valuable" of the remaining services, even though continuing with the same approach means the eventual endgame is a city that provides no services at all.

It's important at this point to ask why cities even exist. After all, what is a city for anyway?

Distilled to its most basic form, a city exists simply so neighbours can cooperate to improve their own lives. By working together, they can achieve more than they could individually. For example, by teaming up with neighbours, we can chip in to pay someone to pick up our recycling and take it to the depot for us. But, alone, we might each have to take it there ourselves.

That's just one example. Another is the fire department. A single resident couldn't afford to own their own fire truck and pay a couple of firefighters to wait on standby in case their home catches fire. Well, okay, maybe a select few residents could do that. But the rest of us need to team up with our neighbours to fund a truck together, and take turns volunteering on shift. Get enough neighbours together, and you can pay people to take those overnight shifts at the fire hall for you.

Same goes for services like libraries, drinking water, or sewage treatment. Maybe your city also owns a park, a zoo or a sports team. No matter what it is, the goal is the same: by pooling our resources together, we can achieve a whole lot more than we can on our own.

Let's take out that first pin now, the one about cities turning a profit like a business.

Because while a city isn't like a business, it *is* like a nonprofit co-op. Its member-owners (citizens) pay annual dues (property taxes) and elect a board of directors (council) to run the co-op with the goal of providing a variety of services to its members.

In this way, cities are able to provide critical life-sustaining services, things like sanitation, public safety and clean drinking water. They can also be made responsible for providing valuable quality-of-life amenities like parks, pools and libraries.

Now, there's no doubt the *value* of city services like those is extremely high. But their *cost* is something else. And for a city to be able to provide these services, essentially, forever, then those costs need to be paid for, not just today, but forever.

Which is why it's important to talk about things like profit in a city. To be more precise, in municipal finance they call it a surplus, but it means the same thing: that you bring in more money than you pay out. Because if you don't, eventually you have to shut down the entire operation. It doesn't matter if you're a business, a nonprofit, a charity, or a city government. If you consistently bring in less than you pay out, you'll eventually reach a point where you're providing no services.

That's why even though a city is more like a nonprofit than like a business, it still needs to earn a profit, er, surplus. The key difference is that for a city, a surplus is a means to an end, not an end in itself.

In other words, cities need to earn a surplus, but not simply for the sake of earning a surplus. They need to earn a surplus so they'll be able to pay for the services they provide, and to do it forever.

Why isn't it enough to break even? We'll get to that. Because, as it turns out, not only do cities need to earn a surplus, but they need to earn *enough* of a surplus.

But we'll come back to that too. For now, I can tell you're still skeptical. Like you've got a burning butfor on your lips.

Which reminds me ... time to take out that second pin.

"But for the fourteen-year tax freeze in early 2000s, the city wouldn't be in this mess!!!"

Look, I can understand why people might think this. I mean, sure, it seems plausible on the surface. But once you start to understand how money flows in a city, you'll see why this isn't the case.

We'll get into the details of why later, but suffice it to say, if the tax freeze was the cause of our financial mess, then we should find absolutely no evidence of financial stress prior to 1998.

Right?

RIGHT??

Chapter 3

It's Like Deja Vu All Over Again

I started writing about city issues on my blog, *Dear Winnipeg*, in December of 2018, but I had been paying close attention to the goings on at City Hall for a few years before that already. After all, I had been witnessing the financial downfall of my city all around me, in actual physical terms, and I wanted to get to the bottom of it. I'm very Nancy Drew like that.

The closure of the Kelvin Community Centre in my neighbourhood in 2007 was a standout. But there were tons of other examples. When I first got involved with our newly formed neighbourhood association in 2016, the group was advocating for new planning regulations for the Elmwood area, to help with stimulating more investment in our community. But we were told we'd have to wait, as the city had no money to pay for that. (No money for city planning? That does explain a few things. But never mind that for now…)

We asked for fix-ups to our area parks. Sorry, no money for that either.

Better sidewalks? Pruning our street trees? Nope and nope.

Additional services and amenities? You're dreaming.

That got us asking, why was there no money to maintain anything around here?

Even as the city had grown in population, as we'd added more taxpayers, somehow we were no longer able to afford the things we once could. How could that be? What kind of donkey auction were they running over there at City Hall?

32 You'll Pay For This!

Side note: my research later revealed it wasn't a donkey auction. It was actually a goat rodeo.

But still, the reason we were given always seemed to be: it's simply a matter of priorities. But that didn't sit well with me. You only need to set priorities when you don't have enough money to maintain everything. If you have enough money to maintain everything, you just do it. No prioritizing necessary.

So how long ago did we start prioritizing due to lack of money? I mean, we know Elmwood Park had a gardener at some point.

As I'm writing this, my news feed has a CBC News article in it titled "Few goodies in store for Winnipeggers as mayor signals stark pre-Christmas budget" in regards to the upcoming 2025 budget.

But it was the same thing the previous budget year: "This is a challenging budget year and so people should expect that difficult decisions are going to have to be made," said Mayor Scott Gillingham at a presser outside his office on

December 6, 2023.

And the year before that, in 2022, even the introduction section of the actual budget document expressed gloom: "We embark on this year's balanced budget update fully aware of the challenges and tough choices that lie ahead."

Here's the thing about writing "a fun blog about infrastructure and municipal finance" for all these years. It means reading a lot of reports, keeping tabs on what's being said in the media, digging deeper into certain planning, transportation or finance topics, in addition to doing a lot of research into past city reports and media coverage, in order to have the necessary context to be able distill often complex issues into fun (ish), useful (ish), short (ish) articles that anyone can enjoy. It can easily take upwards of ten or sometimes twelve hours to research and write each and every one of the letters I post there. So, all told, I've certainly spent hundreds of hours putting together that content.

That's why some things now give me déjà vu. Like the words "difficult decisions" in the context of the municipal budget.

Now, the official reasons have varied from year to year. But regardless of the reasons du jour, it's always felt to me that we've somehow been here before. And it turns out, we have.

And I know what you're thinking... déjà vu, du jour, so many French terms to learn the meaning of! But not to worry. As the grossly underappreciated 2001 cult movie classic *Josie and the Pussycats* taught us, du jour means many things: friendship, family, teamwork, crash positions. Keep that last one in mind as we discuss the city's finances.

Oh, you haven't seen it? Well, it's not strictly necessary to understand the rest of this book. (But if you don't watch it, you'll never know why they're not wearing any hats...)

As we touched on last chapter, here's where people tend to argue that the COVID-19 pandemic and subsequent inflation are at the root of our budget issues. If you're one of those people, it might surprise you to read this pre-pandemic quote in the *Winnipeg Sun* from Scott Gillingham on

March 6, 2020, back when he chaired the Finance Committee:

> Difficult decisions were made to balance the budget. One of the things that this multi-year budget process has shown us is that the city of Winnipeg needs to make sure we are prioritizing those services which are core to our mandate first.

It would be convenient to be able to place the blame on a single person. Convenient, but misguided.

Because before Scott Gillingham, there was Brian Bowman, who as early as the end of his first year as mayor was warning of "difficult decisions ahead." By December 9, 2019, CBC News was reporting that "difficult decisions" had become a mantra for him, as he "uttered the phrase at least nine times Monday morning in a briefing with reporters."

And before him, there was Mayor Sam Katz promising, in his 2011 State of the City address, to "take up the challenge of making the often-difficult decisions that guide, shape and affect the lives" of Winnipeggers.

Of course, all of these came after the fourteen-year-long property tax freeze first championed in 1998 under Mayor Glen Murray. Fourteen years is a long time to go without a tax increase, so it's natural to assume that's where the city's financial issues began.

As it turns out, the tax freeze was in response to Winnipeggers' property tax burden, which at the time was seen as too high.

Because according to the July 20, 1997 *Winnipeg Free Press*, "Winnipeggers already pay the highest property taxes in the country, while enduring pothole-ridden streets and backups from an ancient sewer system. We can't afford to keep all of our kiddie wading pools open, or offer children one free day a week at the Assiniboine Park Zoo. We've slashed the book budget at the public library and reduced library hours. And our taxes still go up."

That's pre-tax freeze, yet it could have been written today. I mean, except for that free day a week at the zoo ... suggesting that today would be seen as outrageously lavish. Kinda like having a gardener in Roxy Park. And yet, we used to be able to afford it.

But council had been having issues keeping our financial heads above water even before that. A quick search through the city archives reveals a 1996 budget motion by Mayor Susan Thompson acknowledging the "difficult decisions proposed."

In 1993, a March 22 headline in the *Winnipeg Free Press* proclaimed "City councillors caught in impossible situation." At the time, we had the second-highest property taxes in the country and spent fifteen cents of every dollar we raised to pay interest on our debt, despite having some of the most efficient municipal services in Canada, spending less per capita on services than most cities our size, and having slashed infrastructure renewal spending to only $7 million (which is just over $13 million today, when adjusted for inflation).

Having the second-highest property taxes in the country was already an improvement. We'd been in the unenviable top spot for such a long time. An analysis done in 1985 by the Toronto-based firm Runzheimer Canada came to the conclusion that Winnipeg topped the country when comparing property taxes, both by sheer dollar amounts, as well as a percentage applied to the market value of our homes. And the September 19, 1985 *Winnipeg Free Press* writes that this wasn't even the first report to come to that conclusion. Yikes!

But we can go even further back to find trouble brewing. A January 6, 1968 *Winnipeg Free Press* article warned of an "inevitable" tax hike, with Alderman Lloyd Stinson calling the constantly rising taxes a "dilemma" and saying that "the only solution lay in a fairer distribution of the tax system." Piling on, Alderman Joseph Zuken felt we also needed a "reassessment of municipal responsibilities."

Though it published it more than a half century ago, the newspaper could simply change the councilmembers' names and reprint the article as is today. As they say in Montréal, plus ça change…

(Sorry, Josie didn't have a translation for that. You'll just have to Google it).

It's Like Deja Vu All Over Again 39

We'll come back to new revenue deals and fairer splits of municipal responsibilities. That really deserves its own chapter.

At this point, it's easy to think that things have just always been bad. I mean, the 1960s is a long time ago. But if you keep going even further back, the references to "difficult decisions" in our budgets just sort of... disappear.

Take this April 4, 1946 headline from the *Winnipeg Free Press:* "A Good City Budget."

If you're not sufficiently impressed by that rare combination of words, you should know the city approved a 10% increase to the tax rate that year.

And people were *happy* about it.

Probably in large part because, as the article stated, "the taxes paid in Winnipeg, per dollar of housing value, may be far lower than is paid in other cities," and that "it is doubtful indeed if the average homeowner anywhere in

Canada pays less than the citizens of Winnipeg for comparable service."

They describe that the new money was needed to pay for increased recreation, a new three-platoon system for the fire department, as well as police, street, sidewalk, and water improvements.

A good city budget? Increasing service levels? No call for a redistribution of the tax burden? Hard to believe we're talking about the same city.

In 1946, at a time when we were just recovering from the Second World War, we decided what services we wanted and then we decided what tax rate we needed to get us there. Like you do when you have money.

These days, we do the reverse: we look at how much money we can raise through taxes, then we decide how many services that will buy us. Like you do when you're broke.

And it's not like it was early in the life of our fair city. In 1946, the city would have been only two years away from celebrating its semisesquicentennial.

That one's an English word, I promise. It means the city was seventy-five years old. And since we just celebrated the city's sesquicentennial, or 150 years, last year, that means things were just peachy from a financial perspective during the entire first half of its life.

So why did the wheels come off in the second half, just like the Bombers in a Grey Cup final?

Clearly, we've identified that there was a time when city finances were good. But since then, even with a growing population, and a growing tax base, we've continued to find ourselves with fewer financial means each passing budget year.

What we're experiencing in Winnipeg isn't unique, it's a widespread North American phenomenon.

But we'll come back to that. Because, if the city is struggling financially like this, why do the bond rating agencies keep giving us high ratings? And what about those budget and financial report awards we keep winning? Don't those mean we're doing just fine financially?

Spoiler alert: no.

Chapter 4

Bond, Municipal Bond

Despite overwhelming physical evidence to the contrary, some people still don't believe the city is in a financial crisis.

Despite the fact that our roads keep falling apart, even with record spending in the last decade.

Despite the fact that we keep dumping raw sewage into our rivers with no ability to pay for the $2 billion upgrades required.

Despite the fact that our parks and recreation infrastructure is currently estimated to cost more to repair than we are able to borrow.

Despite the fact that we've been cutting service levels for decades, all the way back to Roxy's gardener in the 1960s.

Despite the fact that in preparing previous budgets, we actually considered turning off streetlights to save money. We are quite literally "struggling to keep the lights on."

And it keeps getting worse over time.

We know, in our gut, that things are going poorly. We see it all around us.

And yet, some people will point to a letter grade on a random piece of paper as proof that we shouldn't believe our own eyes. Or proof enough, anyway.

So, given all we see around us, and given all the financial knowledge you and I have accumulated so far, how can bond rating agencies keep giving our city a high rating? For example, why would S&P give the City of Winnipeg an AA+ credit rating, the second highest they give?

And more importantly, what even is a bond anyway?

Briefly, a bond is basically just a loan, except instead of borrowing money from the bank, the city is borrowing the money from investors, who are also called bondholders. These investors are often hedge funds, pension plans, or investment banks like Goldman Sachs or Deutsche Bank, who are either investing on behalf of their clients, or sometimes on their own behalf.

They will lend money to a city, and in exchange the city promises to pay it back with interest. Bond is just another word for promise, as in "my word is my bond."

Meanwhile, bond ratings agencies, companies like Moody's or S&P, will examine bond-issuing cities' finances and give them a bond rating. A bond rating is like a credit score, a shortcut that bond investors can look at to get a sense of how likely it is they will get their money back if they lend it to that city.

But here's the thing, in thinking that a good bond rating is a report card for our prudent financial management, we commit a critical error: bond ratings are for investors, not citizens.

In the hierarchy of "who gets paid first" in a city, bondholders are on top. Any money that comes in first goes to them (debt payments), then current city employees (wages), then past employees (pensions), then citizens (services/infrastructure). This is obviously a simplification, but you get the idea: bondholders first, the people of Winnipeg last.

This is true for any corporate structure, whether a business, a charity, a nonprofit, or a municipal government. We, the owners—the members, the shareholders—who elect a board of directors (council), get paid last. So when things go sideways financially, *we* feel the effects first. Maintenance will be neglected, services will be cut, taxes will be raised.

The bondholders, on the other hand, will feel it last. Because as long as there's a library left to close, a golf course left to sell, a streetlight left to be turned off, bondholders will still get their money. And so the bond rating will reflect that.

But that's obviously not a city anyone wants to live in. A good credit rating doesn't reflect whether we have built a nice city to live in. It doesn't even reflect whether our finances are being managed prudently. It only measures whether we have enough liquidity to pay our debts, which is the actual lowest bar we can set as a financial goal.

In other words, the city's credit rating isn't a report card on how well we're doing. It's not even for us, the citizens of the city. It's a tool for bond investors that answers one question, and one question only: "How likely is it that the city of Winnipeg will default on a debt payment in the next twenty-four months?"

In that case, it's not hard to give the city an AA+ because the city isn't likely to default on a debt payment in the next twenty-four months.

But defaulting on debt is not the first sign of financial trouble. It's the last. As Ernest Hemingway wrote, bankruptcy happens gradually, then suddenly.

When a city borrows money, repaying those loans becomes the first priority for any cash coming in. Bond investors don't care if the city has to raise taxes in order to make their debt payments. They don't care if it has to cut services, close pools, abandon bridges or reduce transit service. None of that matters to them.

But it matters to us.

When we're forced to make cuts to transit service, that will have real-life impacts on people's ability to access jobs, schools and other economic opportunities.

When we're forced to make cuts to recreational amenities, that will have real-life impacts on youth development, health outcomes, and potential gang involvement.

When we're forced to increase taxes to a level beyond

what the community can bear, that will have real-life impacts on affordability and quality of life.

Before we suddenly miss a debt payment, we'll have gradually made life worse for everyone in the city for a long time. Decades, even.

Plus, there's a reason bond ratings agencies aren't afraid that we won't miss those payments. This is from Moody's October 2021 credit assessment of the city:
> Winnipeg's rating incorporates Moody's assessment of a high likelihood of extraordinary support from the Province of Manitoba in the event that Winnipeg faced acute liquidity stress.

In other words, the ratings agencies are confident that the province will bail the city out if ever we come close to not being able to make our debt payments.

When your parents are co-signing your loans, the bank is not afraid to lend to you. Even if you can't afford to pay your rent or buy groceries, the bank's not worried about that. It'll get its money, even if it has to go to your parents.

This should have become obvious on July 10, 2015, when Moody's downgraded the province's credit rating. Only two business days later, on July 14, Moody's also downgraded the city's rating, explaining:

> Winnipeg's rating is impacted by the credit quality of the province, with today's change reflecting the marginally lower ability of the province to offer support in the event the city faced acute liquidity stress.

A lot of people at the city were upset about that, blaming the province for impacting the city's credit-worthiness. But how can you argue that a low rating is the province's fault, while a high rating is due to the city's excellent financial management?

And just in case there's still any doubt left in your mind that a good bond rating equals sound financial management, we can go back just a little bit further, to the global financial crisis of 2008. You know the one. The one that was brought on, in part, by ratings agencies attributing high ratings to subprime mortgages and fancy financial products like CDOs. CDOs that were made up of thousands upon thousands of

NINJA mortgages, a term made up at the time to describe loans to people with "No Income, No Job or Assets." They were unquestionably toxic financial garbage, and they were rated AAA investment grade. In the aftermath of the crisis, the ratings agencies even paid fines for having done this, before they went back to business as usual.

It's incredibly obvious to us now that those ratings had nothing to do with the quality of the underlying financial asset. So why would anyone think it's different for cities?

Exactly.

But I guess there's still the nagging issue of the national awards our city keeps winning for its budget and its financial reports. Open up any budget document from the city in recent years, and you'll find mention of a national award our budget has won! In fact, our city budget has won the Distinguished Budget Presentation Award from the Government Finance Officers Association (GFOA) every year since 2019. Pretty cool, eh?

But, it's important to understand what this award is and what it isn't.

What it is: The Distinguished Budget Presentation Award, presented by the Government Finance Officers Association (GFOA), recognizes the city's hard work on the budget. It is the highest form of recognition in governmental budgeting.

What it isn't: a report card on how well the city is doing financially.

The GFOA also gives out the Canadian Award for Excellence in Financial Reporting, for our year-end financial reports, which the city has also taken home every year since 2017. That is also not a report card on how well we're doing financially.

Not to take away from the hard work that our city's financial staff have put in to deserve these awards, but these are not awards for having a great budget and financials. They're awards for having a great budget *document* and financial *report*.

The criteria are things such as these:
- Is there a table of contents?
- Does the table of contents hyperlink to the appropriate pages?
- Does it include a legible organization chart?
- Are individual revenue sources described?
- Etc.

The goal of these awards is to ensure that cities are reporting all the relevant information accurately and transparently so that citizens, the media and council members can make informed decisions based on the financial facts.

And these awards say that, yes, the information is all there. That's not a small feat. So, congrats to the city's finance department on a well-deserved award! Not every city is as thorough.

But just because the information is there doesn't mean the public, the media, and the council members are equipped to understand it. The average financial report from the city is nearly a hundred pages long. And the average budget usually has more than seven hundred pages spread over two volumes!

How do we make sense of all this data at a very high level? How can we get a feel for our city's overall financial trends, so that we know which questions to ask? And how do we do it without having to sort through eight hundred pages of small-print financial documents? And, importantly, how do we do it without needing to be an accountant?

Ideally, the city would produce this type of analysis as part of its annual reporting. That would allow us to spot financial decline before it turns into real-world decline and reverse course.

Unfortunately, we've had to fly blind with respect to our city's financial condition, which has been bad and getting worse for a long time. But the information is all there to show it, and we have the awards to prove it. We just need to learn how to read that information. Because it's not theoretical— we'll be living with the consequences for the rest of our lives. And for that, it'll be useful to talk a bit about municipal accounting.

Chapter 5

There's No Accounting for Taste

Remember how I said that a city not only needs to earn a surplus, it needs to earn *enough* of a surplus, and that we'd come back to it?

Well, welcome back.

Yes, it's going to be that kind of chapter. Better pour yourself a glass of your favourite wine. Don't worry, I'll wait.

Ooh, rosé! Nice choice, all that French in chapter three must have rubbed off on you. Well then, let's dive right in so you can learn a few new accounting terms!

What do you mean, you don't think you can do it? You read the previous chapter on bonds and now you're speaking French and drinking rosé. Learning to speak accounting is not any harder. You can totally do this! Plus, just like French, you'll be pleasantly surprised to see how many words you probably already know!

The first thing to learn is the difference between a **budget** and a **financial statement**.

Woah, those are some mighty huge sips there! Pace yourself, my friend!

Now, a lot of people use the two terms interchangeably, and it's true, they are very similar. The key difference is that a budget is created at the beginning of the year and lays out what the city *plans to* spend, while a financial statement is created at the end of the year and lays out what the city *actually did* spend.

Easy peasy, right?

For now, we'll leave the beginning-of-year budget talk for a later chapter, and just focus on the end-of-year financial statement stuff.

Municipal financial statements have a few major parts to them. One of them is the **statement of operations**. In the business world, they call that part the **income statement** (or the **profit & loss statement**, or **P&L**). All these terms mean pretty much the same thing, so I'll just call it the P&L going forward because it's shorter.

Yeah, sure I can wait while you pour yourself another glass!

Now, the P&L is probably one of the easier documents to understand, as it's basically a list of all the income for the year, minus all the expenses. If you spent less than you earned, then you have made a surplus (or profit, remember?) for the year. Yay!

If you spent more than you earned, then that means a loss. Boo!

Fairly intuitive, right?

It's the part that's most like our own personal finances, so it more easily makes sense in our (non-accountant) brains.

That's why most of the city's public communications is around the P&L. It's why most media reporting revolves around it. And it's why most of the questions from the public revolve around it. Like, why is the library's budget being cut? Or, why aren't we spending more on roads?

But despite all this emphasis on the P&L, the answers we seek live in a whole other place. I'm guessing you've heard of investors looking for a "strong balance sheet" on TV or in movies, like Charlie Sheen's character in *Wall Street*. Although in that movie he's talking about sex, so that's probably a bad example.

That said, have you ever heard anyone talk about a "strong P&L"? Exactly. Because that's not a thing.

There's No Accounting for Taste 59

Despite being the most important part of financial statements, the **balance sheet** is the least understood. It's actually called the **statement of position** in municipal accounting, but I'll call it the balance sheet going forward, like in the business world, because it's one of those terms that is probably already familiar to you.

So what is it? And why is it so important?

Well, the balance sheet is like an up-to-date list of all the stuff you own at the end of the year.

There are four main categories of stuff on the balance sheet. They're laid out in a different order on the page in municipal accounting, but the relationships between them are easier to understand when we lay them out in the same way as we would for a business:

> **Financial assets (cash):** this is money, and stuff that is worth money that could quickly and easily be turned into actual money.
>
> In your own life, this would be cash (whether in the

bank, your purse, or the sofa), your retirement account, that savings bond your grandma bought you for your seventh birthday, and the twenty bucks your co-worker still owes you for a group gift to your boss.

In the case of a city, this means cash (whether in the bank or in the petty cash envelope in the top left drawer of the mayor's desk. Granted, I don't know for sure that's where they keep it. It might be the bottom right drawer...). It would also include things like money held in savings, and any taxes or fees that are owed to the city but haven't been collected yet (also known as accounts receivable).

Capital assets (infrastructure): this is all the stuff that has a long-term use and is still worth money, but that would take longer, and be more complicated, to turn into cold hard cash if you ever had to sell them.

In your own life, this would be your house, your car, the velvet Elvis hanging in your den, and your extensive collection of Beanie Babies.

In the case of a city, this means things like bridges, roads, pools, fire trucks, civic buildings, buses, laptop computers and everything else like it.

Liabilities: this is debt, and any other money that is owed to others.

In the case of a person, this would be your mortgage, your credit card balance and lines of credit, and that $5,000 you still owe your buddy for the Beanie Babies collection you bought off of him in 1999.

For cities, this is municipal bonds, bank loans, lines of credit, wage and pension liabilities, as well as money owed to suppliers and contractors that haven't been paid yet (also known as accounts payable).

Accumulated surplus: this is sometimes called **equity**, or (more precisely) **retained earnings**, in the business world.

In the case of a person, this would be your Net Worth.

If it's negative, that's bad. If it's positive that's good. If it's over a million dollars, then congratulations, you are a millionaire. Also, can I borrow your monocle? For a city, this is simply the running total of all the surpluses and/or losses generated every year since the city was born.

That part is important, so I'll say it again. The surplus (aka profit) the city makes at the end of every year gets added to the accumulated surplus on the balance sheet. The surpluses accumulate there. Again and again, every year.

Now here's the second important point. It's called a balance sheet for a reason.

Cash + Infrastructure = Liabilities + Surplus

The stuff on the left is always equal to the stuff on the right. It's "balanced."

So here's the sneaky part. When a city buys infrastructure,

it doesn't show up on the P&L as an expense. It just shows up directly on the balance sheet.

Sorry, those are the rules of accounting. That's partly why cities separate their budgets into operating and capital budgets, something we'll deal with in a later chapter.

Wait, is that your third glass of rosé?

No matter. You wanna buy a new fire truck, road or pool? No problem, we'll just move some dollars from the cash pile over to the infrastructure pile. And because those two are on the same side of the scale, the balance sheet is still balanced.

And we can keep doing that, funding our infrastructure construction (and let's not forget infrastructure maintenance and replacement), moving money from the cash pile to the infrastructure pile, year after year after year, forever.

Or, at least until we run out of cash.

So then what?

Easy! We just need to get more cash, right?

Well, not so fast. The only way to add anything to one side of the scale is to add an equal amount to the other side. So if we want to add new cash to one side, then we'll need to add an equal amount of either debt or surplus (or a mix of both!) to the other side. And that makes sense when you think about it, doesn't it? If you want to have a new $10 that you didn't have before, you either need to borrow $10 (debt), or you need to earn $10 then not spend it (surplus).

In other words, the money we need for infrastructure will *always* come from either debt, or surpluses, or a combination of both. And in the case of debt, it will eventually need to be paid back. Out of surpluses. But we can talk more about debt later.

What that means is that when it comes to funding infrastructure, it all comes down to having surpluses, eventually. And since surpluses come from the P&L, where we spent less than we made, that's why we need the city to "turn a profit." Every year. Otherwise, there's no money for infrastructure, neither for building new, nor for maintaining the old.

So the real questions is, like we said before, is the city earning *enough* of a surplus to pay for our infrastructure needs? How would we know? And what does that have to do with the gardener in Roxy Park? Those are all excellent questions. And we'll get to them. After we talk about debt.

By the way, you don't look so good. Maybe you should have had the super-fun grape punch instead. I'll try to find my recipe. In the meantime, go lie down for a bit, and we can continue this later.

Chapter 6

Til Debt Do Us Part

Feeling better? Cool, glad to hear it. You probably wouldn't want to talk about municipal debt with a queasy stomach.

Don't worry, you've already learned the hard part. This one will be short and sweet.

So now you understand that operating surpluses are what generate the cash we need for capital spending (aka infrastructure spending). In order to have money on hand this year for roads, fire trucks, or rec centres, we need to have collected operating revenue, like property taxes, in years past *that we didn't spend then.*

Now, let's say we neglected to build up a surplus to cover those future infrastructure costs. There is one other way to come up with money for infrastructure spending in our capital budget: we can also choose to borrow money for those roads, fire trucks, or rec centres. But when we borrow money today, we're agreeing to repay that money in little portions every year after, until all that money is paid back.

And where does the money for those payments come from? That's right, the same place all new money comes from: from operating revenue that we don't spend on services in those future years.

So, in a nutshell, today's capital dollars (paid for with cash) are simply yesterday's surplus operating dollars. And today's capital dollars (paid for with debt) are simply tomorrow's surplus operating dollars.

Let that sink in for a bit.

Yeah. Capital dollars are just operating dollars from a different year.

If you only have one takeaway from this entire book, let that be it. I'll say it again: capital dollars are just operating dollars from a different year.

And that's before we even consider the costs of interest, of actually operating that infrastructure, and of course, of maintaining and eventually replacing it, all of which is also going to come from future years' operating budgets, ultimately. But we'll talk more about that later.

For now, just remember that when we borrow money to pay for infrastructure, we're promising that our future selves will be willing to increase revenues or cut expenses, or both, in the future to pay it back.

Once you understand that, then the rest is going to become super obvious. So congratulations, time to celebrate with a bottle of sparkling wine!

Oh, too soon? Okay fine. But then let me show you how you can predict the future with your newfound skills!

Maybe then you'll feel like celebrating again?

Chapter 7

Back to the Future

As I'm sure you're already aware, despite our best intentions, we humans are notoriously bad at predicting the future. Whether it's the weather, stock prices, or the score of tomorrow's hockey game, there isn't a single person on the planet, much less in the city, that can reliably and consistently predict the future.

Oh, it's not like we don't try.

In 1956, there were 410,787 people living in the Greater Winnipeg area, according to census figures. City planners at the time estimated the city's population would grow to 800,000 by 1981, twenty-five years later.

Someone like Marty McFly, who travelled back in time from 1985 to 1955 to kiss his mom (it's been a while since I saw the movie, the details are a bit fuzzy), could have told those planners they were dead wrong. After all, the population would only turn out to be 564,373 in 1981.

Without the benefit of a time-travelling DeLorean, planners couldn't know that we wouldn't break the 800K barrier until 2023, only forty-two years late! Of course they couldn't, but they pretended they did anyway.

Yet planners aren't the only ones at the city who pass off wild guesses as hard facts received from the future version of Doc Brown. Traffic engineers, economists, and even politicians get in on the game, using their predictions to determine city policy and direct spending decisions. But whether it's predicting population growth, traffic growth, or GDP growth, they're all just wild guesses. Wild guesses that we bet our city's entire financial future on. Yikes!

Luckily, there is one place we can look that will give us 100% certain insight into the future, and that is the city's financial statements!

No, not in the P&L. The P&L only tells us this year's income and expenses, so it can only tell us about the present.

Instead, we need to look at the balance sheet, because it can show us our past, as well as our future. I told you it was the most important part!

Now I know I just finished saying that humans are bad at predicting the future. Notoriously so, even. But the balance sheet doesn't really predict the future. It's more like it brings the future into the present. Consider it our financial DeLorean.

Remember how capital dollars are just operating dollars from another year? And that a surplus is a dollar that comes from the past, while debt is a dollar that comes from the future? That's time-travel, baby!

In a way, we're not really seeing the future. It's just that the future has travelled into the past to become our present, so the future is really the past, and the past is now the present! Just like if your future self went back in time to punch your neighbour and steal credit for someone else's baked in already. The money is already spent. The future is the present.

That's how powerful the net financial position is in telling us about the future. It's so important that the Public Sector Accounting Board mandates that cities in Canada report it directly on their balance sheet. So far, US regulators haven't mandated it, so you could say we're pretty lucky to be in Canada. But as you can see, it's pretty easy to calculate anyway, if you know what you're looking at. Which you do now!

But more important than the net financial position itself is the ability to track it over time. The trend is more important than the number, because where we're headed is more important than where we are. We are time-travellers after all.

But wait, doesn't the city's charter force it to balance its budgets every year?

A balanced budget means we always have more revenue than expenses (or at least equal) in a given year. So if we've had like, 150 consecutive balanced budgets, how did we manage to spend even one dollar from the future, never mind $1.2 billion?

I think you know the answer already, but humour me while I go get my corkboard, thumbtacks and red string.

Chapter 8

The Ghosts of Budgets Past

Stick with me... I promise this will all make sense!

When we talk about the city budget, you've likely heard that it's made up of two parts: the **operating budget** and the **capital budget**.

You may already know the difference between the two, but the Coles Notes is this: in general, infrastructure spending goes in the capital budget, while everything else goes in the operating budget.

If you want a more detailed explanation, it's actually

spending on things that have a value that lasts beyond one year (fire trucks, roads, pools) that goes in the capital budget, while spending on things that last one year or less (wages, fuel, pencils) goes in the operating budget. In general. But that's just for the keeners.

Now, if this reminds you of the P&L and the balance sheet, you're right. What goes in the capital budget at the beginning of the year is generally what will show up on the balance sheet at the end of the year, while what goes into the operating budget at the beginning of the year is (again, generally) what will show up in the P&L at the end of the year.

That's why when it comes to revenue for the operating budget, we get it from things like taxes, user fees and government transfers, while revenue for the capital budget comes from a surplus in operating budgets of other years (either past, in the case of cash, or future, in the case of debt).

Now here's the next level. When you spend in the operating budget, it's a one-and-done type of transaction. You pay the librarian's wages and there's no further commitment (unless you have the librarian work more hours). Similarly, once you've paid to clear the snow, there's no further commitment, unless you have the snow cleared again. And if you hire or fire a pool attendant this year, you can always reverse your decision next year.

That's how we can be certain that the city's fourteen-year tax freeze in the early 2000s— or really any year we've increased taxes by less than inflation—cannot be the cause of today's financial crunch.

The city's charter forces it to balance its operating budget every year. So, if inflation makes our costs go up, we can rebalance our budget in two ways: raise taxes to be able to pay for the same level of services, or cut services to be able to pay for them with the same amount of money. Once we've decided which of those tools to use, that inflation is dealt with. Importantly, it doesn't keep building up over time if we choose a service cut over a tax increase. Once a library hour has been cut, or a gardener has been laid off, its cost to the city is now zero, no matter what inflation does in future years.

And being in the operating budget, it impacts that year's budget, and that year's only, because we can always make the reverse decision next year. Now, if we're needing to make *further* cuts in the operating budget the following year, that's a new, different problem. It has nothing to do with not raising taxes the year before.

But the capital budget is different, because it *does* commit you to future obligations. Once you build or buy a piece of infrastructure (a road, a pool, a bus) in the capital budget, you are now committed to future costs in three ways:

Operations: every piece of infrastructure will have operating costs in order to use it. Pools will need to be heated, cleaned and staffed. Buses will need fuel and drivers. Even roads need electricity for traffic lights, cleaning and restriping every spring, and snow clearing several times per winter. These will come out of future operating budgets.

Maintenance: depending on the type of maintenance needed, these costs may come out of future operating budgets or future capital budgets.

Replacement: every piece of infrastructure will eventually come to the end of its life, and will need to be entirely replaced. This cost will come out of a future capital budget.

Since capital budget dollars are just operating budget dollars from another year, every piece of infrastructure we build commits us to finding all those additional dollars in future operating budgets, beyond the initial cost of its construction. And since the lifetime of most infrastructure is measured in decades, those impacts will be felt in operating budgets for decades as well.

That means the city budget really *is* made up of two parts: the decisions we make today, in addition to the decisions we've made over the past fifty-plus years.

Now, if the infrastructure investments we made in the

past had been productive, in that they actually paid us a return on investment, then we would have the necessary income to cover those additional costs, with enough left over to fund the services we want. The budget discussions we'd be having would be centered around questions such as "which new services should we spend this extra money on?" or "how much of a tax break should we give ourselves?" or "is there a new piece of infrastructure that would serve us well?"

But we'll come back to productive investments in another chapter.

Instead, we're faced with discussions around which services to cut, how much of a tax increase (or user fee increase) to implement, and which infrastructure to neglect. Every budget is simply an exercise in determining how much to allocate to each of those categories.

Sometimes, some of the choices are made for us, like the sudden failure of the Arlington Bridge, or when the mayor pro-actively decides what the tax increase will be, whether that's 3.5% like in recent years, or 0% like in the early 2000s. We're just forced to make up the rest in the other categories.

But none of those decisions address the root cause. These are simply the symptoms of a much greater illness: generations of money-losing infrastructure investments.

(Oops, I talked about it again. I promise we'll come back to that!)

Anyway, that's why, after we do this exercise for the budget one year, we just start it all over for the next budget. We haven't solved anything; we're just dealing with the fallout from our choices over the past several decades.

And more is coming. It's baked right into the process, because we can't change the decisions made in the past. We saw it in the previous chapter with the net financial position. There are at least $1.2 billion's worth of prior mistakes coming down the pipeline.

We just have to deal with them as they work their way through the system. And that will continue for as long as we keep making bad decisions. To actually make progress, we'll need to change our approach to city development.

But I'm getting ahead of myself again. Before we talk about that, let's talk about something else I can tell is on your mind.

You may have heard that cities in Canada are responsible for 60% of all infrastructure while only collecting 10% of every tax dollar. Isn't that the cause of this all? If cities had a fairer split of tax revenues with the province and the feds, all of this would be solved. The city just needs to strike a deal for a new revenue model.

Right?

Not to ruin the next chapter for you, but that's poppycock.

(I've always wanted to use that word in a serious context. I won't lie, that felt so good, I may just do it again.)

Chapter 9

Let's Make a Deal!

By this point, I'm sure you would not be surprised to learn that the City of Winnipeg posted a $377-million surplus in 2023. And $57 million the year before that.

In fact, the city has posted a cumulative total of nearly $3.7 billion in surpluses since 2005. And while that would leave most people scratching their heads as to where all that money went, you already know the answer, you extra-smart municipal accounting superfan. It went where all surpluses go: to infrastructure!

In 2005, the city had spent 97% of all the surpluses it had generated since 1873 on infrastructure. By 2023, it had spent more than 115% of those cumulative surpluses.

Knowing that the city has spent more than all of its surpluses tells us that we'll need to make up those surpluses in the future. In future operating budgets.

As we've seen, that's what the net financial position is. As it's in negative territory, it tells us the city has already spent more money in the past (on infrastructure) than it has brought in, money it will need to make up in future operating budgets. Either through service cuts, or revenue increases. Or both!

Once we've cut services to as low as they can go, the only remaining option is to accept tax increases to make up that money. So it's clear to see that a lack of revenue, for a gardener or for anything else, isn't the cause of the city's problems, it's just a symptom of having overspent on infrastructure in the past.

But how could the city have overspent on infrastructure if everything is still falling apart? If the Arlington Bridge is closed, if Happyland Pool is closed, if our roads are as potholed as the surface of the moon, doesn't that mean the city has underspent on infrastructure?

Well, Dr. Intelligent Slacks, actually it's both. The city has underspent what's necessary to maintain what it currently owns. But it has overspent the money it has available to do so.

So doesn't that prove a need for more revenue? After all, according to the Federation of Canadian Municipalities website, municipalities are responsible for 60% of all infrastructure while only collecting 10% of every tax dollar.

You're right, Professor Clever Trousers. That doesn't seem very fair.

But, as they say, there are lies, damn lies, and statistics. Consider these examples. The province is responsible for 100% of healthcare costs. Does that mean it should be entitled to 100% of every tax dollar? And cities are responsible for zero per cent of national defence spending. Should that mean cities deserve zero per cent of all tax revenues? Of course not, Captain Genius Jeans. It's apples and oranges. It's hogwash, codswallop, flapdoodle, piffle, malarkey. Poppycock, if you will. Just like that infrastructure statistic.

Despite that, it's pretty obvious there's a problem. We can see it all around us: abandoned bridges, closed pools, pothole-riddled roads. Is this really a problem that can be solved with more revenue?

Both the province and the feds are in a deficit position. For cities to get a larger portion of an already-too-small pie means cuts will be necessary elsewhere. So what do you think should get the axe: health care, education, housing?

Alternatively, to increase the size of the pie means creating a new tax (even though there's already nothing preventing city council from increasing property taxes). Many people have proposed new municipal income or sales taxes, for example. Unfortunately, there are several key problems with these so-called municipal "growth taxes." Proponents argue that funding local infrastructure from property taxes is inherently unfair, since they don't automatically grow as the economy does, like sales taxes do. But there's actually nothing preventing council from raising property taxes when the economy grows. That's a political problem, not an economic one. The real advantage of a sales tax is to hide tax increases from public scrutiny, since they happen automatically without any need for council discussion. In that sense, they're just a more opaque local tax, and with less transparency comes less accountability. When city leaders don't need to debate tax increases, they aren't held to defend their spending decisions, leaving less incentive to ensure that infrastructure investments are positive-returning. Given how little attention has been paid to that already, that's a step in the wrong direction.

Still, those might be trade-offs worth considering if sales taxes actually solved the problem. But when looking throughout North America, cities with a local sales tax fare no better than cities without. For example, the California cities of San Bernardino and Stockton both declared bankruptcy despite having some of the highest municipal sales tax rates on the continent.

And if all that wasn't bad enough, "growth tax" is actually a misnomer. Sure, they grow when the economy does, but they decline with the economy too. When a recession inevitably hits, sales tax revenues drop, sometimes precipitously, like during the COVID-19 pandemic.

Cities provide critical life-sustaining services to residents, like water, sanitation, and public safety. Should we be betting our ability to provide clean drinking water on the gyrations of the economic cycle, federal interest rate policy, and unpredictable world events? Such critical services need a stable source of funds to ensure they're never disrupted.

Rather than have the delivery of those services be reliant on the economy, a measure of *community income* that can vary wildly from year to year or even month to month, it would be more prudent to fund them from *community wealth*, which is much more stable over time. And since more than three quarters of Canada's national wealth is held in real estate (77% as of 2022), the best way to access that would be through some sort of tax on those properties. Like a... property tax.

As an added bonus, land is also impossible to hide in

Let's Make a Deal! 91

an overseas tax shelter!

Now all that could still be an argument for a "fairer" split of responsibilities between orders of government. But, before we provide local politicians with a blank cheque, it would be important to ask how much they would need.

Hang on to your quick-witted pantaloons, my friend. It's about to get real.

The infrastructure deficit is a calculation of how much extra money the city will need over the next ten years in order to care for its infrastructure. As of the end of 2024, the city's asset managers have calculated they will need $12 billion to do that. And they've identified $4 billion in available money to do it. That leaves an $8 billion unfunded "gap" that the city will need to find in order to meet its upcoming infrastructure needs in the next decade. That gap is the city's infrastructure deficit.

It comes out to an average of $800 million per year of new money needed. And it's an amount that's been growing for years as the city has fallen further and further behind on its infrastructure obligations.

How much money is that? Well, for comparison's sake:
- the city collected just $752 million in total property taxes in 2024
- eliminating the entire police department, the entire fire and paramedic department, as well as the entire community services department (that's all the libraries, pools, rec centres, etc.) would only save about $620 million per year
- the province's 12.5-cent-per-litre gas tax brings in about $304 million per year (for the entire province)
- each per cent of provincial sales tax brought in $386 million in 2023 (again, province-wide)

In his March 2024 report, *A modest proposal: A plan to give municipalities access to personal income taxes*, David Macdonald, a senior economist with the Canadian Centre for Policy Alternatives, estimated that the city could raise $16 million per year if it was allowed to charge a 1% income tax on individuals in the top income bracket. To get to $800 million, we'd have to charge a 50% tax on the top income bracket, bringing their combined federal-provincial-municipal tax rate to a lofty 100.4%. In case it's not obvious, that would mean paying more than all of their income in tax. Yikes.

Instead of taxing only the rich, if the city were to increase taxes on the rest of us too, Macdonald estimates that every per cent of income tax charged on all but the lowest tax bracket would still only raise about $64 million per year.

Never mind the same ballpark, we're still not even in the same universe! As you can see, the magnitude of this amount is so great that it can't simply be fixed with a tax increase—of any type.

And that's just to keep up with our infrastructure needs *for the next ten years.* It doesn't address the extra money we already know we'll need to find to deal with the negative net financial position that is filtering its way through our operating budgets as those liabilities come due. Which, you'll remember is simply our infrastructure over-spending from the past.

And it certainly doesn't include restoring any services

we've already cut, or adding any new services or infrastructure. The odds of getting that gardener back in Roxy Park are looking bleaker and bleaker ...

Where does that leave us?

Winnipeggers can't afford a property tax increase that would be high enough to bridge this gap. But neither can we afford it as a sales tax, or an income tax, or a liquor tax, or a sewer fee hike, or any other tax.

So while a redistribution of responsibilities might be a worthwhile exercise in order to address governance issues, it won't address financial issues. Redistributing the pieces of the pie between orders of government doesn't create more pie.

Because no matter which order of government collects it, every tax dollar ultimately comes from the same place: our pockets. And it's not that our city can't afford it. It's that *we* can't afford it. No matter how shrewd our chinos are. And this is the case throughout North America.

Our infrastructure deficits are impossibly high no matter

where you go.

Now, we're constantly told that infrastructure spending is an investment in growing the economy, and it is. But, if the previous investments we made had grown the economy the way it was promised, the taxation capacity would exist in the economy, somewhere.

But it clearly doesn't.

Which leads to the common response that we need to grow the economy some more to increase the taxable revenues that will pay for what we've already built. The new growth will pay for the old growth.

Remind you of anything? That's quite literally the mechanism for a Ponzi scheme!

But that's a topic for a later chapter. For now, it's time to talk some more about economic growth. Is it really the silver bullet to addressing a city's financial problems?

Good thing too, I'm all out of synonyms for pants.

Chapter 10

One Free Lunch, Please!

We've danced around it long enough. It's true that the only ways to create the new surpluses our city will need in the future are to cut services, defer maintenance on infrastructure, or increase taxes.

I agree with you, none of those sound amazing.

Except there's a bit of a loophole in the last one. Because tax revenues are a function of two things: the tax base and the tax rate.

Here's a super basic simplification of it. When the city collects property tax from you, they do so based on the value of your house. Same for your neighbours. In the interest of fairness, everyone may pay a different *amount* of tax, but everyone pays the same *rate*.

For example (again, this is simplified), if the value of your house is $250,000 and the tax rate is 1%, you will pay $2,500 in tax (this is a simplification, but you get the picture). But if your neighbour's house has a value of $300,000, they'll end up paying $3,000 since everyone is charged the same 1% tax rate. That's a total of $5,500 collected by the city.

YOU: $250,000 x 1% = $2,500
NEIGHBOUR: $300,000 X 1% = $3,000
TOTAL FOR THE CITY: $5,500

As a city in search of more money, you could increase the tax rate. Ratcheting it up to 1.3% would translate to an eye-watering 30% tax increase for you and your neighbour, making your only two citizens very, very angry.

YOU: $250,000 x 1.3% = $3,250
NEIGHBOUR: $300,000 x 1.3% = $3,900

TOTAL FOR THE CITY: $7,150

But if instead, a third neighbour moved into the city and built a new house for themselves, even a small one valued at a modest $165,000, the city could keep its tax rate stable at 1% and still bring in a total of $7,150 in tax revenue.

YOU: $250,000 x 1% = $2,500
NEIGHBOUR: $300,000 x 1% = $3,000
NEW GUY: $165,000 x 1% = $1,650
TOTAL FOR THE CITY: $7,150

That's growth in action! And growing the tax base is the other way we can increase tax revenues without increasing the tax rate charged to everyone. In fact, if the tax base grows enough, there are cases where we could even reduce the tax rate on everyone and still bring in more money than before.

Well, cities are wise to this. It's why city leaders always seem so focused on growth: growing the city, growing the economy, growing the tax base.

When you're strapped for cash, it's a great way to increase revenues without upsetting everyone with a tax rate increase.

Of course, there's no such thing as a free lunch.

Or is there?

No, there isn't.

Those new homes or businesses need services. And they'll need roads to reach them, and pipes so their toilets can flush.

And even if the developer pays those initial infrastructure installation costs, which are ultimately passed down to the buyer, the maintenance, operation and completely predictable eventual replacement of that infrastructure becomes the responsibility of the city.

So even though there's new revenue coming in from this new growth in the tax base, there are also new expenses.

That's why it's important to make sure that there's *enough* of that new revenue to cover all the new expenses.

For the services on the operating budget side, that's pretty easy, because, as we saw, those are all in the present. This year's revenue needs to be higher than this year's expenses. Blammo, done!

For the infrastructure, it gets a little more complicated. Especially since none of that shiny new stuff will even need any maintenance or replacement until many years in the future. It's still brand spank. But eventually it will need maintenance. And replacement. Not just once, but in repeating cycles forever. And the tax base needs to be able to pay for it.

And there it is again: a reminder that a city not only needs to earn a surplus, it needs to earn *enough* of a surplus.

It might help to think of it this way: infrastructure, from a financial perspective, behaves very much like debt. When a city borrows money, it comes with a future financial liability, an obligation to pay at a later date. We know when, and how much.

Similarly, when a city builds a piece of infrastructure, or a developer builds it for them, it also comes with a future financial liability, an obligation to the citizens of that city to maintain and repair it, of course, but also to eventually completely replace it when it comes to the end of its useful life. And to replace it again every time it comes to the end of its life after that.

Forever.

From the moment we build something, we already know that one day, we'll have to replace it. And through the magic of Asset Management Planning, we can even know when, and how much it will cost. Just like with debt.

So if it looks like a debt, and it quacks like a debt, shouldn't we treat it like a debt? We obviously can't take on an infinite amount of debt without compromising our ability to meet our future obligations to repay it.

But is it different with infrastructure? Since building infrastructure tends to incentivize new development around that infrastructure, therefore growing the tax base, can we just go out there and build an infinite amount of infrastructure, and then bask in the warm glow of tax base growth? Can we assume that more infrastructure is always better, because it also helps grow our tax base?

Well, would we spend a trillion dollars to build infrastructure if it only grew our tax base by a single dollar?

No, of course not.

So, if a trillion-to-one isn't it, then what *is* the ideal ratio for new infrastructure? Because remember, the new infrastructure should create enough new tax value not only to provide services to those new areas, but also to replace itself, continually, forever. And furthermore, if that ratio exists for new infrastructure and its newly created tax base, then surely it also applies to existing infrastructure and the current tax base.

Sounds like something cities should be paying close attention to.

Because here's the kicker ... infrastructure is like debt, except a lot worse. When debt comes to the end of its term, we pay it, and that's the end of it. But when infrastructure comes to the end of its life, we pay to replace it, and then the clock just resets and starts over again. It's like a never-ending zombie debt.

And yet, we haven't ever bothered to calculate the maximum amount of zombies our tax base can handle. Shouldn't we do that?

Chapter 11

Night of the Living Debt: Revenge of the Zombies

Okay, calculating how much infrastructure our tax base can afford is going to be a big job. Luckily, a lot of very reputable researchers and organizations have done some of the heavy lifting for us.

One source is the Federation of Canadian Municipalities (FCM). In 2023, they released research, *Canada's housing challenge is also an infrastructure challenge (FCM)*, that showed that, on average, each housing unit in Canada needs $107,000 of municipal infrastructure.

If that sounds like a lot for your household to be responsible for, I should probably highlight that that's an average. Like we saw in the last chapter, property taxes are collected in a pro-rated way based on the value of your home.

So, not to freak you out, but there's a very good chance you're actually responsible for *much more* than that.

(If you're wondering what "responsible for" means to your wallet, I'll get to that.)

If you add up the assessed value of every property in Winnipeg, to give us the city's assessment base, or tax base, you get $131 billion as of the end of 2024.

The last time the city published a replacement cost for its infrastructure in 2018, it was calculated at about $35 billion. Adjusting for growth and inflation would put it somewhere in the ballpark of $46 billion today. That makes the ratio of tax base to infrastructure somewhere in the area of 2.8 to 1.

And that's catastrophic. Why?

Let's look at it this way: according to the Winnipeg Regional Real Estate Board, the average sale value of a detached house in the city in 2024 was $423,878. For condominiums, it was $274,201.

If you live in a house assessed at $423,878, a ratio of 2.8 to 1 means your "share" of Winnipeg's infrastructure is over $150,000. And the average condo-dweller is still responsible for $98,000.

And just in case you think renters get a free pass, they don't, since their rent ultimately pays their landlord's property taxes.

Now, being "responsible for" this much infrastructure doesn't mean the city would ever send you a bill for $150,000 or even $98,000 all at once, or at least we hope it wouldn't.

No matter if the city is trying to save up surpluses for the next infrastructure replacement, or if it already did it using debt and now has save up surpluses to repay that debt, it collects that amount in smaller chunks over several years through property taxes. If we assume infrastructure needs to be replaced every twenty-five years on average, that would be $6,000 per year. If we stretch it to fifty years, that's still $3,000 per year in property taxes.

And that's just the money we need to collect for infrastructure replacement only. It doesn't include maintenance yet. Or any services like police, fire protection, snow clearing or garbage pickup. Our taxes currently cover the costs of those services, but they don't even come close to funding our infrastructure replacement.

If we added those costs in, we'd be looking at tax bills that are much, much higher than today. In fact, just the infrastructure replacement portion (that we should be collecting, but aren't) is already a lot more than the entire property tax bill of a given property today. This isn't a couple of percentage points, it's orders of magnitude higher.

Whether the city collects it through a property tax, an income tax, a sales tax, or some sort of user fee doesn't matter. And like we saw earlier, whether the city pays for it, or the province or the feds do it doesn't matter either. All of it ultimately comes from the same place: our pockets.

The problem isn't so much who's collecting the taxes or how, but rather that those who are paying them, us, don't have enough to give. After all, it's not like there's hundreds of millions of dollars sloshing around in the local economy just waiting to be taxed.

The bottom line is we've built way more infrastructure than the size of our tax base, our economy, can support.

But wait. We're always told that infrastructure spending is an investment, which it is. And that it grows the economy, which it also can.

And yet we've just finished five years of "record spending" on infrastructure only to find that our infrastructure deficit has worsened from $6.9 billion in 2018 to $8 billion today. All this record spending was largely fuelled by increasing debt, continuing a well-established trend. In the last fifteen years alone, our city has more than tripled its long-term debt, from $397.5 million in 2007 to over $1.41 billion in 2023.

Per person, that works out to an increase from $608 per Winnipegger to $1,730 in the span of just fifteen years. And that's just the long-term debt. When we include all the city's liabilities, we've gone from $1,235 owing per person in 2007 to $3,501 in 2023. This, despite having added 160,000 new taxpayers to share the load!

Why then, if infrastructure investment is so good for the economy, are we finding ourselves with fewer and fewer means to provide services every year, despite steadily growing the tax base?

Like, how is it even possible to have too much?

Well, when it comes to infrastructure, as with all investments, it's too easy to forget that there are good investments and bad investments. And if the investments we've made in the past have only served to dig us deeper and deeper into debt, then those are bad investments.

Remember that FCM infrastructure research that said every household in Canada is responsible for an average of $107,000 of municipal infrastructure? That's an average of all the municipal infrastructure that exists using the current pattern of development in Canadian cities. The per person amount would likely be similar in the US because cities in Canada have just copied their development patterns from our American cousins. But not all types of development need the same intensity of infrastructure.

As the very same FCM research points out, a 2023 study of the metro Vancouver region, *Costs of Providing Infrastructure and Services to Different Residential Densities (Metro Vancouver Regional Planning)*, determined that the costs for onsite infrastructure for a single-family house in new developments are five to nine times higher per person than for multi-family developments in established neighbourhoods.

And, according to a 2021 study commissioned by the City of Ottawa, *Summary Update of Comparative Municipal Fis-*

cal Impact Analysis (Hemson), servicing low-density homes built on previously undeveloped land on the edge of the city *costs it* $465 per person every year, over and above what it receives from property taxes and water bills, while high-density infill development provides the city with $606 of *net profit* per person each and every year.

To recap, some development patterns are a net drain, and some generate a net profit. We'll talk about this more later.

Let's go back to that infrastructure deficit of ours, where we have $12 billion of infrastructure work to do in the next decade, but only $4 billion identified to pay for it.

If we had a third of the infrastructure that we have today, we wouldn't have an infrastructure deficit. Because instead of $12 billion of infrastructure work to do, we'd only have $4 billion. And we have $4 billion of money lined up already.

If we had a quarter of the infrastructure, not only would we not have an infrastructure deficit, but that would also free up an additional $100 million per year of revenue so we could increase services (gardener, anyone?), build new stuff, or even reduce our taxes!

What kinds of things become possible if we had a fifth to a ninth of the infrastructure?

For that, we need to see what changed in our approach since we last had a gardener tending to the lily pond in Roxy Park. Since there even was a lily pond in Roxy Park.

But before that, let's zoom out a bit to see what happens when cities build more infrastructure than they can handle.

Chapter 12

All Bezzle, No Steak

I first came across the word "bezzle" in the summer of 2022 while reading a really interesting article about Uber's financial statements, on Canadian-British author, activist and journalist Cory Doctorow's personal blog, pluralistic.net ("Uber's Still Not Profitable" August 5, 2022.). In it, he predicts the eventual inevitable demise of the company, because, as he states, "every bezzle ends." It had me asking myself the obvious question, what the heck is a bezzle?

Although it sounds like a pizza seasoning, bezzle is actually a word coined by Canadian-American economist John Kenneth Gailbraith in his 1955 book about the 1929 stock market crash, appropriately (if not obviously) titled *The Great Crash, 1929*. It's derived from the word embezzlement, which he thought was "the most interesting of crimes."

You see, with embezzlement, unlike most other types of theft, there's a delay between the time the crime takes place, and the time the victim discovers the crime. Because of this, there's a period of time where the total amount of money thought to exist, what Gailbraith calls "psychic wealth," is higher than the total amount of money that actually exists ("real wealth").

For example, let's say you have $100, and a fraudster has none. There's a total of $100 of real wealth in the system. Once the fraudster has stolen your money, but before you discover it's gone, the fraudster now has $100 (and knows it), and you still think you have $100. So both of you are going about your lives thinking, and acting, like you each have $100. The total amount of money thought to exist, the total "psychic wealth" is now $200, even though the actual "real wealth" is still $100.

All Bezzle, No Steak 115

That extra $100 is called bezzle. Fake money that is thought to exist, but actually doesn't. Because eventually, every bezzle ends. At some point, you'll discover the fraud, realize that you actually don't have the $100 anymore, and the psychic wealth will return to match the $100 of real wealth. But of course, money (fake or real) can't just disappear without someone feeling the pain of it ... in this case, you. This is important to remember: when bezzle ends, someone always pays.

So what does this have to do with city finances?

Well, hold on to your shizzle my dizzle, because this is where it gets interesting.

While Gailbraith invented the concept of bezzle to describe fraudulent activities, like embezzlement and Ponzi schemes, it wasn't until the 1990s that Charlie Munger, aka Warren Buffett's long-time business partner at Berkshire Hathaway, expanded the concept to apply to stock markets and the wider economy. In a November 10, 2000 speech to the Philanthropy Roundtable in Pasadena, California, he explained that fraud wasn't even necessary to create bezzle, that it could be created in the wider economy whenever asset prices rose higher than the real earning capacity of those assets.

In other words, whenever stock or real estate prices rise higher than what they're really "worth," bezzle is created. We call these stock bubbles, or real estate bubbles, or asset bubbles, but in all cases, it has the same effect: people feel richer temporarily, so they spend and borrow as though they actually are richer.

But because every bubble bursts, and every bezzle ends, eventually someone gets stuck with the bill, driving home the realization that the added perceived wealth wasn't real at all.

But it goes even further than that. Because all that bezzle-fuelled additional spending tends to boost GDP, the artificially bezzle-boosted GDP can lead to the creation of even more bezzle, which pushes GDP up even further, continuing up in a self-reinforcing cycle.

But every bezzle ends. Sometimes quickly, in a blazing financial crisis that forces individual asset owners to take huge losses personally, stuck with high levels of debt and no assets to cover them. Sometimes slowly, like with government bailouts of large banks, where the loss is spread out over many years and paid for by taxpayers, directly through taxes, or indirectly through inflation, recession and unemployment. Sounding familiar? With bezzle, someone always pays, and usually, it's us.

As Michael Pettis, non-resident senior fellow at the Carnegie Endowment for International Peace, professor of finance at Peking University's Guanghua School of Management, and an expert on China's economy, puts it in an article on Carnegie Endowment's website ("Why the Bezzle Matters to the Economy," August 23, 2021):

> Unfortunately, the history of bezzle suggests that, while ordinary households and workers absorb few of the benefits from the creation of bezzle, they tend to absorb most of the costs of its reversal: it is probably not just a coincidence that periods in which large amounts of bezzle are created and then destroyed seem

almost always to experience rising income inequality.

How does this apply to cities? Patience, we're getting there.

We've seen how bezzle applies to fraud, and we've seen how it applies to asset bubbles. But Michael Pettis goes on to describe a third variation on bezzle, which he says "in some cases can be by far the largest source of bezzle in an economy." And he calls that source "Bridges to Nowhere."

Examples he cites are Japan's infamous, and literal, bridges to nowhere, as well as China's entire economy, for which he claims as much as half the GDP growth in the recent past may be due to bezzle creation.

As he explains it, any time a government builds any kind of infrastructure, from roads to bridges to factories, that doesn't have enough real economic growth to support it, then you have created bezzle. And every bezzle ends.

It doesn't take a huge leap to see how that applies to cities in North America. Charles Marohn, president of the US nonprofit Strong Towns, explains it as follows in a 2016 article on their website:

> Most American cities find themselves caught in the Growth Ponzi Scheme. We experience a modest, short-term illusion of wealth in exchange for enormous, long-term liabilities. We deprive our communities of prosperity, overload our families with debt, and become trapped in a spiral of decline.

"Ponzi scheme," "illusion of wealth," "spiral of decline." Marohn is describing the prevailing pattern of development since the 1940s not just in Winnipeg, but pretty much everywhere in North America. But these words also describe exactly the stages of bezzle creation, of temporary increases in psychic wealth, and the end of that bezzle.

And every bezzle ends. Always.

But we'll come back to that.

Unfortunately, most people, including politicians and media, are not accountants. And like we've seen, most people intuitively understand the city's operating budget (or P&L)—revenue minus expenses equals net surplus—easy! It's why the focus of most city finance discussions are around the operating budget.

But bezzle isn't created in the operating budget. It's created in the capital budget, on the balance sheet, by our infrastructure choices. And ours have been akin to a Ponzi scheme, our own version of "bridges to nowhere."

That's why it's critical for all of us to understand that the money for capital budgets comes from operating budgets from other years, and that every capital dollar spent, or given by the province or the feds, or donated by developers in kind, commits the city to spending additional operating dollars in the future. It's important so we can see whether we're creating real wealth over time, or just bezzle. Because when bezzle ends, we are the ones who pay.

It's why business investors look for a "healthy balance sheet," and not a "healthy P&L." As we've seen, you can have decades of consecutive balanced/surplus operating budgets, and still get poorer, if you've been creating bezzle instead of creating real wealth.

All Bezzle, No Steak 121

And it's probably obvious to you by now, based on the city's balance sheet, which one we've been doing.

It's also why what we're facing today, and a lot of what we'll face in the future, is already baked in from our past infrastructure choices. Today is just yesterday's future. We can't undo those choices, but we can see their effects coming and plan for them. The sooner we adopt a more productive way forward, the better off we'll be. Because, as always with bezzle, the larger the bubble gets, the harsher it will feel when it pops.

We can ask ourselves, why is there no money to fix the potholes, maintain our rec centres, keep libraries open, invest in transit, care for trees? Where did it all go?

The answer is, while we could have been creating real wealth over the past several decades, instead we've just been creating bezzle.

And every bezzle ends. The only thing left to decide is how harsh we will let the correction be.

Chapter 14

What Happened to Chapter 13?

It was yet another victim of budget cuts forced by our bad decisions haunting us from the past. Typical.

While I have you here, I almost forgot that I promised you some super-fun grape punch. Why don't you whip up a batch right now? You've definitely earned it!

And maybe share some with Connor? I suspect he's getting mighty thirsty…

Recipe for Super-fun Grape Punch

Ingredients
2 liters grape juice, white or purple (your choice)
1 liter pineapple juice
2 liters ginger ale
Frozen fruit (for garnish and to keep your drink cold)

In a large punch bowl, gently mix grape juice, pineapple juice and ginger ale. Garnish with floating pieces of frozen fruit. Feel free to serve with ice cream (to cut the sweetness). Enjoy with your favourite book on city finance!

Chapter 15

Connecting the Dots

By now, I think we've established that our city has way more infrastructure that it can ever hope to maintain. More than *we* can ever hope to maintain.

And that enormous liability is slowly eroding the city's ability to provide even the most basic services. We've seen it all in black and white on the balance sheet, which you are now an expert at understanding!

But before we start closing more pools, rec centres and civic buildings, we should note that 88% of our infrastructure is just the roads and pipes, according to city reports.

And the quantity of roads and pipes we need isn't a fixed amount. It's entirely determined by how we grow our city. In other words, its development pattern.

A development pattern is what describes the way we lay out our city, what we build where and how people travel within it.

Before the Second World War, the prevailing development pattern in Winnipeg, and throughout North America, was one where most people walked to get to where they needed to go. You still had cars, and horses, and bicycles, and public transit, but walking was the dominant way people got around. Because of this reality, we tended to put homes and businesses close together, since humans don't usually want to have to walk any further than they have to.

Building uses also tended to evolve and intensify over time, as needs and demographics changed, as community wealth grew or as the economy lagged, and as new technologies emerged.

This arrangement made our infrastructure investments, particularly the most expensive like roads and pipes, naturally efficient, since putting so many things within walking distance for the sake of human comfort also meant the roads and pipes could be shorter. And therefore, much less expensive.

After all, the roads are there to connect the places together, and if the places are closer together, you don't need as long a road to do it. And it's the same for the pipes, which connect all the places in the same way as for roads, but for toilets.

It's why, as city reports show, we went from having 2,012,800 feet of water pipe servicing 290,540 residents in 1941 (that's 6.9 feet per person), to a whopping 11,911,360 feet for 705,244 residents (16.9 feet per person), sixty-five years later.

Each Winnipegger today is responsible for nearly 2.5 times more feet of water pipe than Winnipeggers in the 1940s. Multiply sewer pipes, land drainage pipes, and roads in the same way, and you can start to see why we can no longer afford our city.

Some might call that a sprawl vs. infill argument, but that's grossly over-simplified. Cities have always expanded outward as they grew in population.

Further, prior to the Second World War, our neighbourhoods were able to evolve. The way we used to develop pre-WWII was through the efforts of thousands of residents and small developers, each adding their contribution to an area, in different sizes, qualities, and at different times.

And as new residents arrived, as businesses thrived, and as local wealth increased, it's these differences that provided the economic incentives to continue improving and investing in the area, sometimes by adding onto an existing building, sometimes by replacing it entirely.

Smaller buildings made way for bigger ones. Older ones made way for newer ones. And shoddy ones made way for nicer ones. Not all at once, but over time.

And as new buildings went up, previous existing buildings became old, creating even more new opportunities.

Values in the centre of the city would go up to a point where they started creating comparatively cheaper opportunities on the edges, which in turn would then start to develop using the same incremental pattern. The more time went by, the more this virtuous cycle of investment continued. Rinse. Repeat.

This traditional development pattern was refined over millennia of iterations of human trial-and-error. Whatever didn't work simply failed and went away, while whatever did work got to stick around and live through another iteration. Successful cities were the result of many, many projects happening continuously. It was resilient, and it created wealth. Today, we might call it "incremental development" and "mixed use infill," but back then we just called it "how you build cities."

Compare that to the predominant development pattern we use in North America today, which started in the 1940s.

In this new development pattern, we now have relatively few large developers developing acres upon acres of land with similar buildings, of similar quality, and most critically, all at once.

This new development pattern is also largely built around moving people in private vehicles, which uses much more land, not only for the roads, but for the parking, pushing buildings further apart, increasing the length of pipes and roads needed to connect everything.

All at once, such a new neighbourhood is willed into existence. And since everything is new, there are no further economic opportunities for development. It is "built out."

Not that you could develop it further even if you wanted to. Even though the tax base created isn't large enough to pay for the infrastructure it needs to exist, we've implemented zoning rules that make it difficult, if not impossible, to build anything else in these existing places. The rules prescribe that what is there is what will always be there, and cannot evolve.

But because, in this (relatively) new development pattern, an entire neighbourhood is all built at the same time, it'll all get old at the same time. And while a crappy, old building surrounded by an otherwise thriving neighbourhood is an opportunity for value-creation, a crappy, old building surrounded by other identical crappy, old buildings is not. And since by this point all the buildings belong to thousands of different owners, it's nearly impossible to redevelop this on a big scale again.

And so faced with this decline, those who can move do, and the big developer starts over in a new location, on the new edge of town. The old neighbourhood nearer the middle has lost value, while the developer creates new value on the edge. But that isn't actually new value at all. It was just old value moved from the centre to the edge. And it comes with additional infrastructure.

This is how, over the past eight decades, our city footprint, and therefore our infrastructure liability, has expanded outwards at a rate that outpaced the local wealth created. The post-WWII development pattern lets existing neighbourhoods decline by design. Then we build new again on the edge with additional infrastructure.

Rinse. Repeat.

All the while, we keep propping it up with ever-increasing debt and maintenance deferral, cutting services and raising taxes along the way. That is how a city slowly goes bankrupt.

The trap, from the city's perspective, is that this new development looks mostly profitable in its early years. And if you are only focused on the P&L, that's all you'd see.

That is, until around year twenty or twenty-five, when all that "free" infrastructure the developers built for us in that development starts needing replacement. At which point we realize there isn't enough money to repair all that infrastructure.

Not to worry, we can just build another round of new development that will generate the additional tax revenue that we so desperately need! We'll just use the new growth to pay for the old growth.

Like we've already seen, that's exactly the mechanism for a Ponzi scheme.

And it's something that's happened to nearly all cities in North America.

While we can keep the scheme going for a while with increasing debt, deferred maintenance, and a combination of service cuts and tax increases, after a few decades of thinking we're doing everything right, it eventually becomes painfully obvious that our city has built more infrastructure than we can reasonably afford. And no amount of new growth will help us. In fact, each additional iteration we build is actually making things worse. Eventually we reach a point where we can't afford new growth while simultaneously needing it.

That's the point we're at today.

If you've ever wondered why, as our population has grown, as we've added more taxpayers, we've had to keep cutting existing services, and leave more and more of our infrastructure to crumble, this is it.

The issue we face isn't a "spending problem," nor is it a "revenue problem." It's an insolvency problem from decades of unproductive investment in a development pattern that returns less than it costs. Under this pattern, "growth" is bankrupting us. But "no growth" would do the same.

For nearly eight decades, we've been investing in a development pattern that costs more to maintain and service than it returns in taxable economic value. And when the chickens came home to roost along the way, we just doubled-down on another round of outward expansion using the same unproductive infrastructure patterns, hoping the new growth would pay for the old growth. And again, and again.

In trying to improve our collective fate, all along we've been looking in the wrong place, the P&L, and inadvertently making things worse. By trying to cut and tax our way out of trouble, we're simply treating the symptoms while letting the underlying disease run rampant.

But by looking at, and understanding, our city's balance sheet, we can start to see where we've gone wrong in the past, and chart a way forward for our future.

Instead of continuing to invest in an infrastructure-heavy development pattern by enabling more car-centric, segregated-use, all-at-once-to-a-finished-state greenfield growth, we need to invest in an infrastructure-light development pattern by enabling walkable, bikeable, transit-friendly neighbourhoods that allow gradual intensification through mixed-use infill.

Not because we have some preference for it, but because those are the profitable investments for a city. More services, and more value, for less infrastructure liability.

Of course, that much is obvious to those of us who understand the municipal balance sheet. It can tell us the future. But the future is not necessarily immutable. And it's never too late to start shifting our approach to avoid an ever-worsening future. After all, I'm still hoping to have a gardener in Roxy Park again in my lifetime.

Chapter 16

Welcome to the 1%!

You did it! You read an entire book on municipal finance and it didn't kill you. Okay, Chapter 5 might have felt like it *almost* killed you, but as they say, what doesn't kill you, only makes you regret drinking all that rosé!

Jokes aside, I do sincerely want to congratulate you. Because you now know more about municipal finance than 99% of people in North America. More than most in the public, in the media, and even on council.

That's no small feat.

But, as Spiderman's uncle once told him, "With great power comes great responsibility."

Being a municipal finance expert (relatively, at least) means it's your job to help others understand it now. Talk to your friends, your family, your colleagues and even your city councillor about this stuff, because it matters. If you're an introvert not up to the conversation, why don't you just give them an easy-to-read book on the topic? Couple it with a bottle of rosé, and it makes a great gift!

As we've seen together, knowing this stuff matters because cities provide valuable quality-of-life amenities for everyone in a community, like pools and libraries and parks (hopefully with gardeners!). And that's on top of the critical life-sustaining ones like clean drinking water, sanitation and public safety.

A city that isn't financially sustainable, one that doesn't generate *enough* of a surplus, year after year after year, will eventually stop providing those services. Maybe not all at once, but slowly and surely over time.

And that's bad for everyone.

Understanding how the balance sheet works is key to understanding that *how* we build and grow our city matters. A lot.

It helps us to see that some development patterns are good for the city financially—they contribute to a "strong balance sheet," helping us pay for more and better services—while others are akin to a Ponzi scheme. Understanding this financial aspect can help inform the bigger picture of all kinds of policy choices throughout the city.

Understanding the balance sheet means we need to get higher returns from our investments, or in other words, a better ratio of tax base to infrastructure. What that looks like in the physical world is building more city on less land, while using less infrastructure.

Yes, that means intensifying the development in our neighbourhoods, allowing for single family homes to be replaced with duplexes, triplexes or fourplexes over time.

But it also means more people getting around on foot, on bike and on transit, the modes that require less infrastructure for the same goal: moving people around the city.

To achieve that, we need to make these trips safer, more convenient, and more pleasant so more people choose them. We can do so by reducing vehicle speeds where people walk (which increases safety while also reducing noise levels), widening sidewalks, adding street trees for shelter, building protected bicycle lanes, adding more public seating to rest or tie a shoe, and clearing snow more quickly on sidewalks and bike lanes.

We also need to put destinations closer together so those trips are easier to make. That happens by allowing small-scale businesses like cafes and hair salons to exist mixed in with our residential areas, and by reducing parking requirements, minimum building setbacks, and lot coverage limits, so buildings aren't forced to be as far apart from each other. Likewise, we can allow housing to be built in commercial areas, so people can live close to their jobs and close to the services they use on a regular basis.

All of these things do two things simultaneously: they cost less in infrastructure investment than the status quo alternative, and they also create more taxable value where infrastructure already exists. We're making better, more productive use of what we've already built, instead of adding to the problem.

Importantly, this means we'll have to embrace small but continuous change. We didn't get here overnight, so we can't expect to be able to reverse eight decades of damage overnight either. But as they say, the best time to start was eighty years ago, the next best time is now.

If our aim is to grow into a financially sustainable development pattern, one that makes efficient use of its infrastructure investments and grows our community's wealth over time instead of eroding it, we'll have to make different decisions on land use, infill, public transit, bikes, recreation, traffic speeds, street trees, and public spaces.

We'll need to see how these components, and more, impact our city's balance sheet, how they fit into a financially sustainable city. In other words, we need to accept and embrace what a financially sustainable city looks like in the real world and make the appropriate choices.

Because the purpose of a city is to provide services to its residents to increase their quality of life, it must have its finances in order to be able to do so. And we need to know, for certain, that it can keep providing all those services not just today, but tomorrow, and the day after tomorrow, and the day after that. For us, for our children, for our children's children. Forever.

Now, get out there and use your newfound superpowers for good. We wouldn't want that spandex outfit going to waste!

Author's Note

To this day, I remember a conversation with my brother-in-law from 2016. My wife and I were talking with him about things happening in our inner-city, downtown-adjacent neighbourhood of Elmwood: the closure of the Kelvin Community Centre, a recent attempt by a pawnshop owner to open up next to a payday lender, the state of our local park, potholes, the Dutch elm disease that was starting to ravage our street trees, and just what seemed like the general decline of our city, which we had been assured by the powers that be was "growing" and thriving. It sure didn't look like it to us.

But he had been reading a blog on city issues called Strong

Towns, and he suggested we give it a look. It was a lightbulb moment for me that inspired me to dig into my city's finances to see what could explain the things I had been seeing all around me. Having been a serial entrepreneur since my early twenties, I had taught myself accounting years ago. I mean, not totally by myself. My dad worked in finance for credit unions for years, and my mom was the CFO for the rural municipality I grew up in. So I had a wealth of financial know-how at my fingertips.

By the time of the October 2018 referendum on allowing pedestrians to cross Portage and Main, our premiere downtown intersection, after four decades of prohibiting it, I was already neck-deep in the city's balance sheets. It was obvious to me that making it easier to walk in the heart of our downtown was a no-brainer. Making better use of cheaper infrastructure while promoting economic activity in one of our city's most productive areas—what's not to like?

When the votes were tallied with a resounding 65/35 split in support of leaving the intersection closed to pedestrians, I knew what I had to do. By December 2018, I had started DearWinnipeg.com, which I called a "fun blog about infrastructure and municipal finance" with the goal of educating my fellow Winnipeggers on the aspects that really mattered in our city's financial statements, and how they affected the decisions we should be making about land use, transportation, trees, sewage—basically everything a city does!

I never expected that it would find a readership from outside my own city, but as it turns out, the challenges we face in Winnipeg are common to so many other places. Today, hundreds of thousands of readers return time and again to read my "fun blog," and 60% of them come from places other than Winnipeg.

It's so great to know that what I have written, on the blog and in this book, is having a positive impact in so many places. But none of it would be possible without so many people in my circle. Of course, a huge thank you to my aforementioned parents, Cyrille and Louise, who got me started with an interest (and dare I say a knack?) for financial issues.

Author's Note

Next up are my brothers, Roger and Réal; my sister, Lise; my friend, neighbour and curling buddy, Antoine; and my brother-in-law, Norm, for always being willing to chat about boring, er— "fun," infrastructure and city finance stuff.

Also, to my wife, partner, and editor, Emma. Thanks for reading, re-reading, and re-reading again, and for being such an inspiration in bringing about positive change in our neighbourhood and our city. Every. Single. Day. I love you!

Finally, to all of you who saw a book on municipal finance and decided, "I'm going to read this!" You're a special kind of person, and we need more people like you, the kind who are interested in working towards a better city (even if your city isn't Winnipeg).

Now, let's get to work!

Recommended Resources

If this book inspired you to dig deeper into this topic, and you don't know where to start, here are a few of my recommendations:

Books

Strong Towns: A Bottom-up Revolution to Rebuild American Prosperity by Charles L. Marohn

The Death and Life of Great American Cities by Jane Jacobs

The Economy of Cities by Jane Jacobs

Antifragile: Things That Gain from Disorder by Nassim Nicholas Taleb

The Black Swan: The Impact of the Highly Improbable by Nassim Nicholas Taleb

YouTube Channels
Not Just Bikes
Ray Delahanty | CityNerd
Strong Towns

Blogs, Websites and Substacks
Dear Winnipeg by me! ;)
Fix Your City by CityShapes
Through the Cobwebs by Brian Pincott
Strong Towns (yes, again!)